The Little Light Shines Bright

A True Story about the World's Longest Burning Lightbulb

---

by

JULIETTE GOODRICH

AuthorHouse™
1663 Liberty Drive
Bloomington, IN 47403
www.authorhouse.com
Phone: 833-262-8899

This book is printed on acid-free paper.

ISBN: 978-1-4343-6524-8 (sc)

Library of Congress Control Number: 2008910144

Print information available on the last page.

Published by AuthorHouse 04/20/2022

authorHOUSE

DEDICATION & ACKNOWLEDGEMENTS

Dedicated to My Three Children
Taylor, Kendall and Cameron

Illustrations: Roseanna Lester
Book Design: Desirée Acosta
Art Concepts: Dionne Egisti
Photographer: Dick Jones
Webmaster : Steve Bunn
Livermore Lightbulb Centennial Committee
Livermore-Pleasanton Fire Department

Cameron stared at his night light too excited to go to bed. All he could think about were fire engines painted bright red.

Finally, the big day arrived! Cameron was on his way. He was going to visit fire station 6, where fire trucks stay.

Cameron had so many questions for the firefighters, so many things he wanted to know.

STATION 6

What if there was a fire, would he get to go?

When Cameron rang the fire house bell, he was greeted with a smile. "Hello, I'm the Fire Chief. You and your parents are welcome to visit for awhile."

Inside the fire house something caught Cameron's eye. It was a little light in the corner hanging up high. The Fire Chief told Cameron, "The light's been burning since 1901, it's older than you and me and most everyone."

Cameron kept admiring the little light shining bright. He couldn't believe it's been on all these years... all day and all night!

The Fire Chief took out a timeline from the start of the light and explained it's been on since before the first airplane flight.

The Fire Chief told Cameron, "The little light has seen it all...

the invention of trains, planes and automobiles....even the first telephone call!"

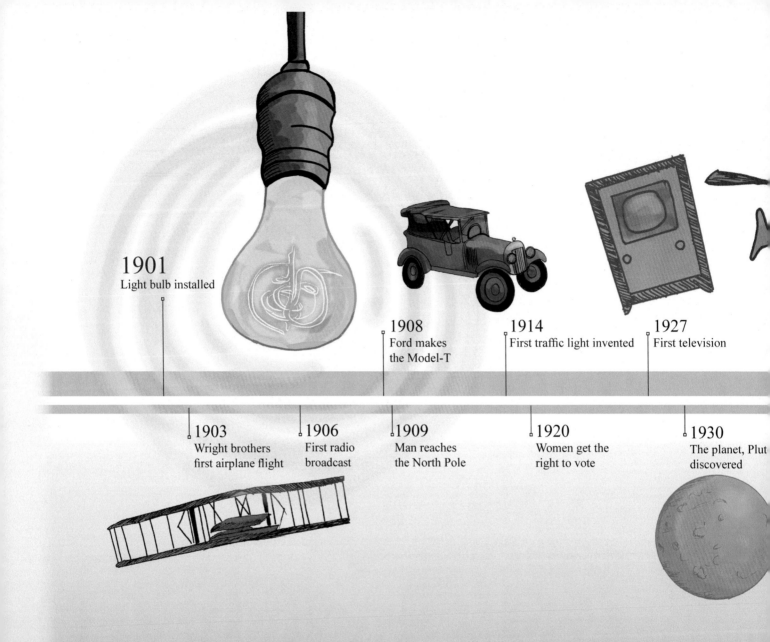

1901
Light bulb installed

1908
Ford makes
the Model-T

1914
First traffic light invented

1927
First television

1903
Wright brothers
first airplane flight

1906
First radio
broadcast

1909
Man reaches
the North Pole

1920
Women get the
right to vote

1930
The planet, Plut
discovered

In 1901 the light bulb was installed, when it celebrated 100 years, the Centennial Light it was called.

1936
First helicopter
invented

1946
First microwave

1955
Disneyland opens

1956
Video tape
invented

1942
Scuba gear
invented

1950
First credit card

1954
Transistor radio
invented

1957
Sputnik satellite
orbits

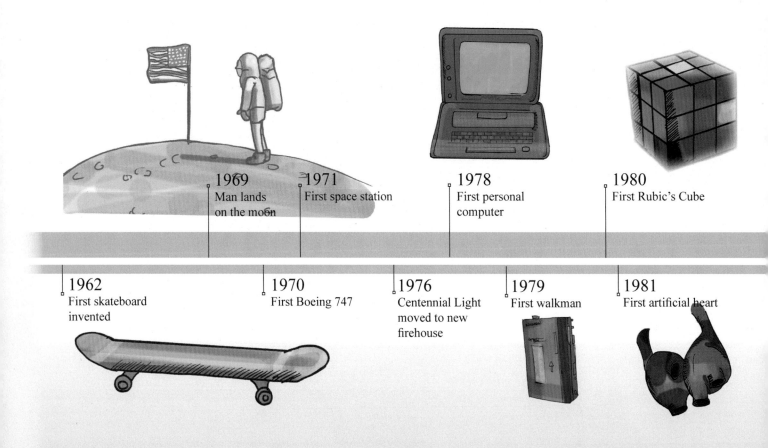

1969
Man lands
on the moon

1971
First space station

1978
First personal
computer

1980
First Rubic's Cube

1962
First skateboard
invented

1970
First Boeing 747

1976
Centennial Light
moved to new
firehouse

1979
First walkman

1981
First artificial heart

"Is it the world's longest burning light bulb?" Cameron wanted to know. The Fire Chief said, "Yes, even the history books say so."

1983
First satellite TV

1990
World wide web

1995
First hybrid vehicle

1989
First Game Boy

1996
Livermore Public Fire
Department formed

2001
Centennial Light
100-year anniversary

One time some firefighters were throwing a ball and almost hit the light right off the wall! "Luckily," said the Fire Chief, "the light kept shining bright. To be honest with you," he said, "it gives all of the firefighters a lot of comfort at night."

"Thank you Fire Chief," said Cameron, "for all you have done. My visit to the fire house has been so much fun!"

That night when Cameron was getting ready for bed, he remembered something the Fire Chief said. "Cameron, when you close your eyes to go to sleep at night, think about fire station 6 and its light shining bright."

STATION 6

Just the thought made Cameron smile and helped him sleep tight. When he closed his eyes, he thought about his new night light.

CENTENNIAL LIGHT
The World's Longest Burning Lightbulb

CAN YOU FIND THE LIGHT?

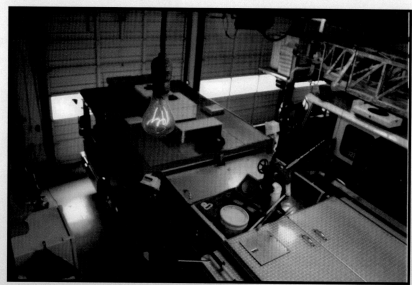

FACT SHEET:

Age: 108 years and counting as of 2009

Installed:

The Centennial light was first installed at the Fire Department Hose Cart House in Livermore, California in 1901. Shortly after it was moved to the main firehouse on Second Street. In 1903 it was moved to a new firehouse and was off for one week.

During it's first 75 years it was connected directly to the 110 volt power line and not to the back up generator for fear of a power surge. In 1976 it was moved with a full police and fire truck escort to its present site at Fire Station 6 . It was then hooked to a separate power source at 120 volts with no interruptions since!

Proof of Longevity:

The light was donated to the fire department in 1901 by Dennis Bernal who owned the Livermore Power and Light Company.

Vital Statistics:

The 4 watt lightbulb is a handblown bulb with carbon filament. The light has been left burning continuously in the firehouse as a nightlight over the fire trucks.

HISTORY OF THE CENTENNIAL LIGHT

Recognition:
In 2007 the lightbulb was declared the oldest known working lightbulb by Guiness Book of World Records.

Future Plans:
The City of Livermore and the Livermore-Pleasanton Fire Department intend to keep the bulb burning as long as it can. If the bulb ever burns out Ripley's Believe-It-or-Not has requested the lightbulb for its museum.

Visiting:
You can visit the lightbulb depending on the availability of the firefighters at Fire Station 6. Go to the rear of the station and ring the firehouse bell. You can also see the bulb if you look through the firehouse window. It's located up high in the left hand corner.

Celebration:
The City of Livermore, The Livermore-Pleasanton Fire Department, The Livermore Lightbulb Centennial Committee and hundreds of guests celebrated the lightbulb's 100th birthday June 8, 2001. Photos available on the centennial light website at www.centennialbulb.org .

BULBCAM
You can see the light in "real time" anytime at centennialbulb.org!

LOOK EVEN CLOSER...THE LIGHT SAYS ON!

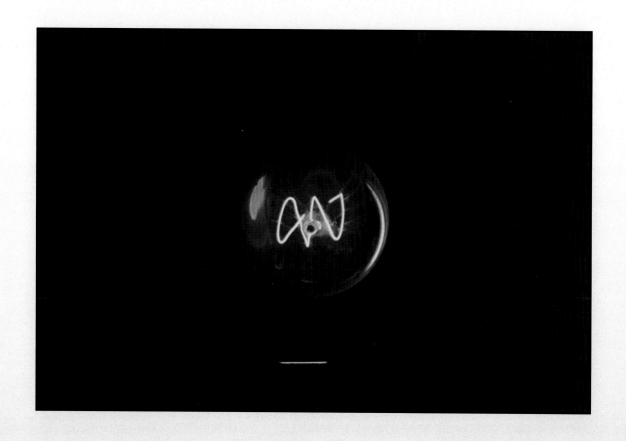

STAT

CAPTAIN 1276

LIVERMORE-PLEASANTON

LPFD

This fire headquarters building
is dedicated to the memory
of the volunteer firefighters
who protected the communities
of Livermore and Pleasanton
from fire for over one hundred year

Printed in the United States
by Baker & Taylor Publisher Services